Utopian Government and Economics

Travis Wayne Goodsell

In accordance with the Copyright, Designs and Patents Act 1988,
Travis Wayne Goodsell exerts his right to be identified as the author of this work.

Copyright © 2016 Travis Wayne Goodsell
Cover Photo © 2016 public domain.

All rights reserved under International and Pan-American
Copyright Conventions.

ISBN-13: 978-1539358145
ISBN-10: 1539358143

www.travis-wayne-goodsell.weebly.com

For you shall know me by my completed works.

Table of Contents

Introduction……………………………...4

Utopian Government…………………...6
    Executive……………………………7
    Legislative…………………………..8
    Judicial……………………………...9
    Human Rights……………………10
    Societal Laws……………………..11
    The New Constitution…………...12

Utopian Economics…………………...14
    Basic Needs……………………...15
    Economic System………………..21
    Business Structure……………....25
    Local Planning…………………..27
    Buildings…………………………28

Introduction

Utopia is the name coined by Sir Thomas More from his book, <u>Utopia</u>. It is his understanding of a perfect society. Others have called it by different names, such as Atlantis, Zion, Nirvana, Eden, and Paradise. There have been those who have written books about it, such as Karl Marx's, <u>The Communist Manifesto</u>, composed songs about it, such as John Lennon's "Imagine"; and there have been those who have tried to build it, such as Adolf Hitler.

My vision of Utopia started at an early age. In 8th grade I had a class with a replacement teacher. He didn't teach us anything, but instead had us create our own perfect society. We had to make a government, economic system, and a geographic map. It was the perfect assignment for me.

After that experience I tried to make a board game in which one tries to create the perfect society. The complexities involved made it nearly impossible for me, until I came across the PC Game Civilization III by Sid Meyers. The instruction book is titled Universal Civilization.

This book covers the four areas of an Utopian society. They are government, economics, religion, and language. In essence I am creating a perfect society. Every aspect that I can conceive of and how to make it function is in this book. As a consequence I have developed some new ideas, such as my hierarchy of basic needs and my universal language.

Probably everyone likes the idea of their own version of Utopia; it's just that there are conflicts and fears about clashing visions. No society on earth has obtained Utopia. And that is probably its allure.

Utopian Government

Executive

The executive in a Utopian society is to function as a diplomat. To give an Executive, executive powers as a third check and balance is too much power to be vested in a single individual. To have Veto power is too much power for one person to wield. But to be able to submit Bills to the Legislature would be more desirable.

This executive pattern is to be patterned at a world level, a national level, a State or Province level, a City level and a Local level.

<u>Legislative</u>

The main body to develop the Law. What I don't like is porking and committees. One Bill, one item per Bill needs to be discussed at a time.

A Council of 50 should suffice to manage the legislative affairs.

This legislative pattern is to be patterned at a world level, a national level, a State or Province level, a City level and a Local level.

Judicial

This check is to decide whether or not the Laws passed by the Legislature are in harmony with a Utopian society. There are two groups. One group is to check the bills of the Legislature and the 2nd group is to decide lawsuits that have risen up the ranks in appeals.

This judicial pattern is to be patterned at a world level, a national level, a State or Province level, a City level and a Local level.

Human Rights

A Utopian society needs a statement of human rights. This protects the people from corrupt government.

Human rights include:
1. Life
2. Liberty
3. Property
4. Basic necessities
5. Freedom from a policing force
6. Fair trial for any and all accusations
7. Fair representation in trials for defense and prosecution
8. To labor in one's chosen field
9. Privacy
10. To Protect life of self and others
11. To Protect liberty of self and others
12. To protect property of self and others
13. The age to be considered an adult
14. Etc.

Societal Laws

A Utopian government needs to establish societal laws to set up its organizational foundations. This is performed at the Local and City levels. These laws consist of those governing the basic necessities, such as traffic regulations.

The New Constitution

Now that we've discussed the elements of a government a Constitution is needed to sum it all up. A new constitution would need to be ordered by category and by administration. All amendments of a category are to be ordered in a numbering system with subsystems identified by a dot, in line with the category, rather than have an amendments section. For the administration the organization needs to be discussed along with the qualifications and duties of each officer. Just like bills are of one subject, so too is the subjects of the Constitution.

The pattern of the Constitution for the World is to be followed by each Nation, each State or Province, each City, and each Local Society. No lesser Constitution has the authority to override a law of a higher Constitution. And the World Constitution is to be the

Supreme Law of the World and the Pattern to follow. Each lesser Constitution is to have as its first statement that the World Constitution is the Supreme Law. Every facet of government and human rights are to be had in the World Constitution. Societal Laws are designed for Local and City Societies. Administrative Laws are the primary concern of State or Province and National Constitutions.

There should be peace in the world, but because there will always be those who seek for power, each level is to provide a military, not a policing force!

Utopian Economics

Basic Needs

Food

   Food is in everyone's hierarchy of needs, such there needs to be an agricultural system involved in the economics.

Clothing

   Clothing is in everyone's hierarchy of needs. Clothing manufacturing is therefore needed in the economic system.

Shelter

   Shelter is in everyone's hierarchy of needs. The level of society determines the level of shelter. For the population growth of the world as a united 1st world society we must build up.

Communication

Communication is essential whenever more than one person is introduced in a society. This involves not only language and writing, but the mediums used to communicate and express ideas and information.

Transportation

Transportation is more essential the larger a society becomes. The need to get to a marketplace and other basic necessities requires greater distances requiring something more than legs for walking, but vehicles for transportation.

Energy and Fuel

The higher functioning the society the greater the demand for more sophisticated the type of energy and fuel. Solar power is the recommended ideal.

Health and Wellness

The need for medical care for prevention and treatment of illness is a necessity.

Education

The more educated a society the higher functioning they are.

Government

The need for the protection of rights requires a system of governmental order.

Religion

A balanced society needs a moral compass.

Love

For the propagation of the species, for companionship, and for affection makes love a necessity.

Income/Property

Also considered a basic right is the ownership of property, or at least an income from some type of economic system in order to obtain property is necessary.

Savings

Not just of income, but of property for an inheritance and for replacement if property gets lost, damaged, etc.

Nature/Plant and Animal life

A thriving society needs vegetation and animal life, especially in a metropolis.

Arts and Entertainment

Beauty and amusement are also necessary features of a society.

Economic System

There are a lot of different types of economic systems. A Utopian world economic system needs to take care of all of its people, but not function as a welfare state. All able-bodied persons must labor for the cause of Utopia. For a world economic system a more elaborate system than just central marketplaces is needed. A World Complex Center is required to supply the deficiencies of the National Complex Centers, which supply the deficiencies of a State or Province Complex Center, which supply the deficiencies of a City Complex Center, which then supplies the deficiencies of a Local Complex Center.

Everyone capable of working labor to supply the Centers, not just to satisfy the Local Complex Center, but to provide an excess to supply the higher Centers in order. So a Local Complex Center labors to supply it with as many different basic necessities that the local society can provide. A Local Society will have a specialty basic necessity(ies) and cannot be expected to produce every single basic necessity or even each variety within the basic necessity. Excess production and manufacturing is necessary to provide the City Complex Center first, so that it can distribute goods and property to the other Local Complex Centers in its jurisdiction.

One Local Society cannot be expected to take care of the needs of one particular basic necessity for the whole world. As such basic necessities need to be made at as many Local Complex Centers as possible so as to provide for the needs of the world.

When the primary basic needs are met, then a variety of basic needs can be performed, produced, or manufactured. Once, for example everyone is provided with a basic level of food, then Local Societies can provide restaurants as a change in variety.

Under such a system, there is no need for money or income. The economic system is run by labor and the larger the world society the more the likelihood that each individual can labor in a field they choose and enjoy, so that there is no forced labor. If there is a deficiency then volunteers can be asked for until production is at a surplus, then everyone can go back to their chosen profession. Variety is a sign of a more developed social structure.

Children, the elderly, and the disabled are thus taken care of by the Local Society in which they reside. They are not able to labor and shouldn't be punished from, or deprived of, their basic necessities. The Local Society need to see to it that goods and property are taken to them.

People are to receive according to their needs, but also according to their wants. Whatever job they choose to help contribute to society with, requires the tools and goods necessary for the functioning of that particular job or hobby. The more jobs and hobbies that a person can perform the greater a contributor they are to society. But no one should be compared to another, but rather each perform what they are capable of.

Greed and selfishness would be eliminated from the individual, for everyone will be focused on caring for not just the Local Society, but as many societies as possible. And in so doing they receive what they need and what they want. And there would be on individual value of goods, not an economic value, such that gold does not have a market value, but intrinsic value to the possessor of the property, which is available to anyone who wants it. This eliminates coveting and theft.

Business Structure

There is the need for Harvesters and Miners of raw materials. These raw materials will then be available at the Centers, but also to Production and Manufacturing Centers or Individuals who have the skill or education in the trade. For example gold is needed to be mined, but then there is a need for a jeweler.

At these types of jobs it is necessary to have an administration to oversee operations and organize and educate the labor. The job would best be served by one experienced in the particular job, rather than someone merely educated in administration.

Individuals can work as a harvester, miner, producer, or manufacturer either at a Center of operations or from their own residence. A person can have a vegetable garden, a honey comb, and be an author of children's books all at the same time.

The Complex Centers are also in need of administration, but also laborers to transport goods between Centers and to warehouse the goods.

Local Planning

A well planned Local Society will best utilize the resources of the land and zone it for its use. Housing will need to be in easy transportation range of the Local Complex Center as well as business centers. Solar powered mass transit is ideal for transport not just to the different types of Centers in a Local Society, but to the City Complex Center and from there to the higher up Centers.

Buildings

A step pyramid style building structure will work best to provide sufficient room necessary to perform the job functions, but also for residing and to provide vegetation surrounding the building at each level. Water storage for rain and snow collection can also be had at each level. The water stored can be used for irrigation and plumbing. In this way a water treatment plant would supply buildings for drinking, bathing, and cooking and cleaning; which the used water can be stored and used for irrigation and plumbing as well. The capstone can be a four-sided solar panel to run the building in conjunction with a solar plant. And wherever possible, robotic technology is to be used to avoid make-work labor and allow people to pursue their passion.

www.ingramcontent.com/pod-product-compliance
Lightning Source LLC
Chambersburg PA
CBHW071835200526
45169CB00018B/1528